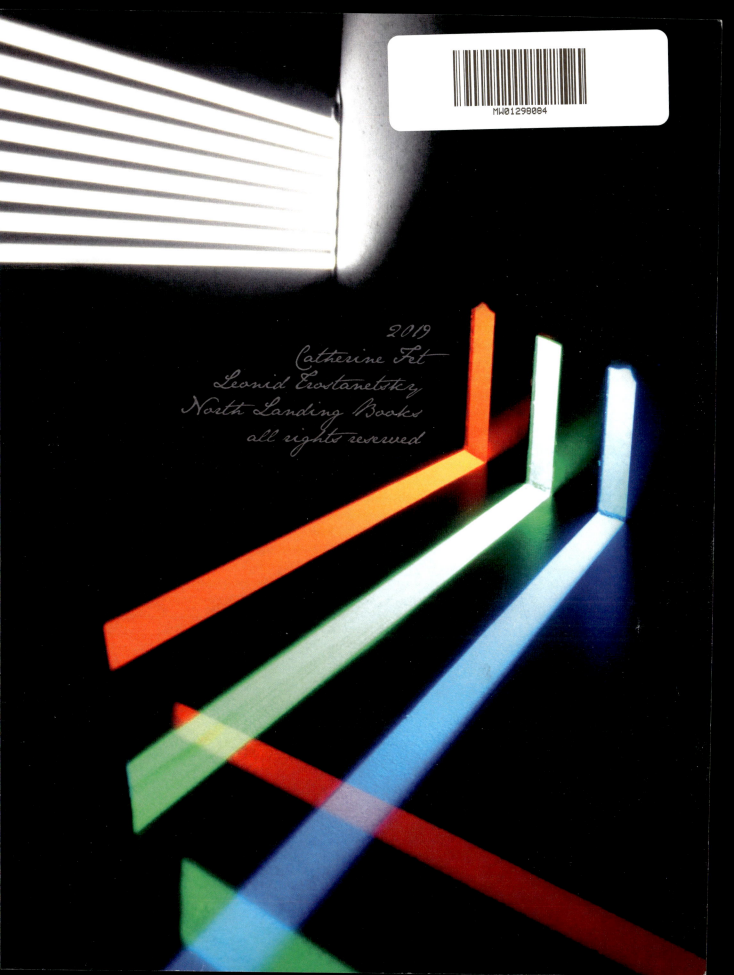

What Makes a Rainbow?

A rainbow happens when it is raining
in one part of the sky and sunny in another.
The colors of the rainbow are
Red, Orange, Yellow, Green, Blue and Violet.

English scientist Isaac Newton explained
how a rainbow forms. He shined light through a **prism**.
A prism is a crystal or a glass object with polished facets.
When the light passes through the prism, it splits into rainbow colors.
Suddenly, Newton saw a rainbow on the wall. He called it the **spectrum**,
which means a ghost in Latin! Scientists use the word **spectrum**
when they talk about light and color.
So why does a prism split white light
into rainbow colors?

White light (like sunlight) is made of
colored light. When all the colors mix,
they make white light. Light is made of
tiny bundles of energy called **photons**.
A stream of photons acts as a **wave.**
Different colors of light have
different **wave lengths** and
different photon energy.

white light

Here is a light spectrum,
with the violet light on one end and red light on the other end.
Violet light has the shortest wave length. Its photons have the highest energy.
Red light has the longest wave length. Its photons are low-energy.

So when white light hits a prism, the prism bends the path of the photons.
Because the energy of the photons is different for every color, light waves of
different colors leave the prism in slightly different directions.
That's how white light gets split into a rainbow of colors!

Light of shorter wavelengths is bent the most.
That's why red, with its long wavelength is at the top
of the rainbow, and purple is at the bottom.

When it rains, each rain drop becomes a tiny prism.
When the sunlight enters a raindrop, the light colors separate,
and we see a rainbow.

Is it possible to get to the end of the rainbow?
No. When you move, the rainbow moves too, because it takes
distance to see millions of raindrops all splitting the light
together. Also, the sun must be behind you.
When the sun is lower, in the morning or in the evening,
the rainbow will be higher in the sky.
And when the sun is higher, the rainbow will be lower in the sky.
In winter we don't see rainbows because raindrops
freeze into snowflakes.
The science that studies light is called **Optics**.
It's a branch of **Physics**.

Make Your Own Rainbow!
Cut a narrow window in a paper rectangle, and tape it to a glass full of water. Make sure the light shines through this window onto the top of the water. Look! Now there is a rainbow on the table!
To make the rainbow brighter, I hold a sheet of paper behind the glass.

Why Do We See Colors?

white light

reflected light

To see color, you must have light.
Remember, white light is made from a mix
of colored light. So when a ray of white light
shines on an object, it's actually
a bundle of colored light mixed together.
In this bundle, some colored light bounces off
the object. It is **reflected.** And some light
disappears into the object.
It is **absorbed** or 'eaten up' by the object.
Our eyes see only the colors that are
'bounced off' or reflected.

So if a lemon reflects yellow light,
and absorbs all other colored light, we see it as
yellow. And if a pomegranate reflects red light,
and absorbs all other colored light, we see it as red.

When you see a blue flower,
what color light does it reflect?
That's right: Blue light!

What is going on when
you see a white object,
like a white sheet of paper?
The paper looks white to us because it reflects
all color light equally, and does not absorb
any colored light at all.
What about black objects, like a black cat?
A black cat's fur absorbs all colors equally,
and does not reflect any colored light at all,
so it looks black to us.

Artists call black a color, but for scientists black is when there is no color, because all colored light is being eaten up by a black object.

In optics, the colors red, green, and blue are called the **primary colors of light**. Other light colors are mixes of red, green, and blue.
The word **primary** comes from the Latin word **primus**, which means 'first'.

red, green, and blue, or RGB primary colors →

But artists have a different color system. For them the primary colors are red, blue, and yellow, because red, blue, and yellow paints cannot be mixed from other colors. In this art color system, the colors that can be mixed from two primary colors are called **secondary** colors.

← *red, blue, and yellow primary colors*

Artists use a color wheel to learn about primary and secondary colors.
Colors opposite each other on the wheel are called **complementary colors**. If you want two colors to look great together, choose complementary colors!

color wheel

complementary colors: pink and green, blue and orange ←

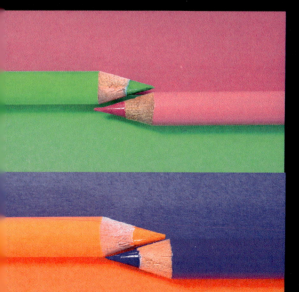
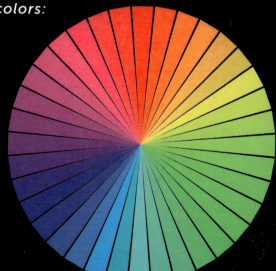

Why Do Things Look Darker When They Are Wet?

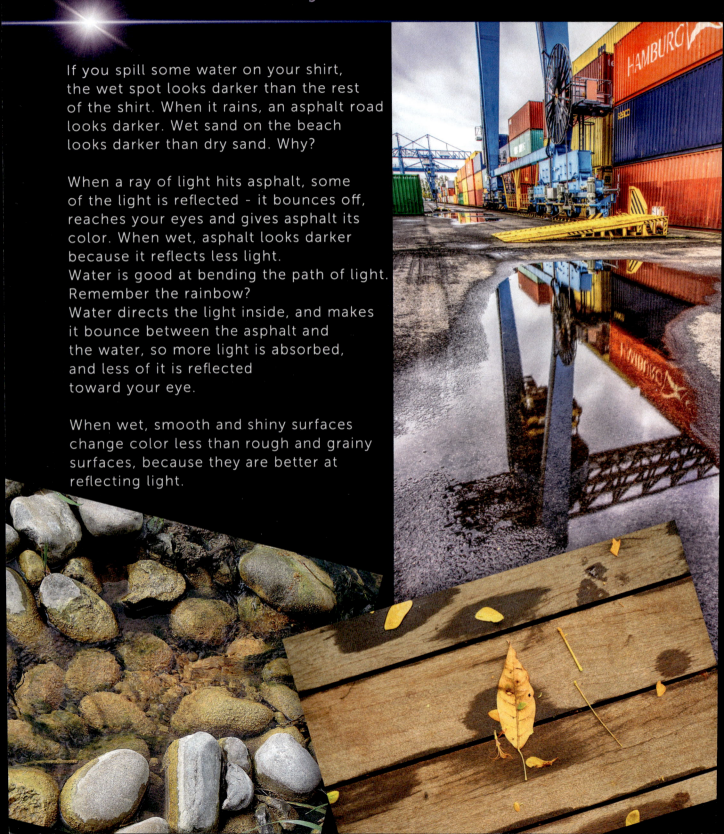

If you spill some water on your shirt, the wet spot looks darker than the rest of the shirt. When it rains, an asphalt road looks darker. Wet sand on the beach looks darker than dry sand. Why?

When a ray of light hits asphalt, some of the light is reflected - it bounces off, reaches your eyes and gives asphalt its color. When wet, asphalt looks darker because it reflects less light.
Water is good at bending the path of light. Remember the rainbow?
Water directs the light inside, and makes it bounce between the asphalt and the water, so more light is absorbed, and less of it is reflected toward your eye.

When wet, smooth and shiny surfaces change color less than rough and grainy surfaces, because they are better at reflecting light.

Why is the Sky Blue?

If sunlight is white, why is the sky blue? When sunlight approaches the Earth, it hits the Earth's atmosphere. The **Atmosphere** is the blanket of air and clouds covering our planet. When photons of sunlight enter the atmosphere, their paths are bent, just like when the light enters a crystal prism. The atmosphere works as a giant prism. It splits a lot of white light (but not all of it) into rainbow colors, and those colored beams are reflected by air, raindrops, and dust in the atmosphere.

Colored light of short wavelengths, such as blue and violet, is reflected more than the light of longer wavelengths, such as red and yellow. The blue and violet rays are scattered all over the atmosphere, so we see blue light coming from every direction in the sky. That's what makes the sky blue!

What about violet light? Why isn't the sky violet? Human eyes do not see violet light as clearly as they see blue light, because violet light is less bright than blue.

Why is the Sky Red at Sunset?

In the daytime we see the sun high in the sky.
To reach our eyes, sunlight comes straight
down through the Earth's atmosphere.
At sunset the sun is low, just above the horizon.
To reach our eyes the rays of sunlight
have to travel along the surface of the earth:
That's a longer path.

The atmosphere of the Earth is a blanket of air,
clouds, and some dust. It slows down
white light and breaks it into colored light,
like a prism. The colors of shorter wavelengths,
like blue and purple, are scattered around and
have a hard time reaching our eyes.
The longer the light has to travel,
the less blue light we see.

But red light has the longest wavelength,
and it reaches our eyes, even if it has to travel a longer way.

That's why the evening sun looks more red as it approaches
the horizon. The clouds reflect this red light, mixing it with other colors,
so we see pinks, oranges and reds. And we also see some purple
in the areas where the blue of the sky mixes with the red of the sunset.

The colors of the sunrise are usually lighter than those of the sunset.
More pink than red. And that's because in the morning the air is cooler, quieter,
and cleaner than in the evening. There is less dust in the air, and less air movement,
so more blue light reaches our eyes, and the sky looks less red.

Why Do Diamonds Sparkle?

When diamonds are found in diamond mines, they look like transparent rocks. To turn these rocks into diamonds, facets are cut into them. **Facets** are smooth flat surfaces. The facets turn dimonds into prisms! Light enters a diamond from the top, gets trapped inside, bounces off its facets, and splits into rainbow colors! Then both rainbow and white light are reflected back out, toward our eyes. That's what our eyes see as shiny and sparkling.

diamond rock

A diamond's shape has to be just right to create the most sparkle. If it is too deep or too shallow, a lot of light is lost.

The angles between diamond facets have to be just right too. If they are not perfect, the light won't split into rainbow colors.

One of the most important things about a diamond's cut is its **symmetry.** Symmetry means an object looks the same on two or more sides. For instance, a butterfly is **symmerical**: Its two sides look like mirror reflections.

round diamond facets

view from the top bottom, and side

A snow flake is symmetrical on 6 sides! It has 6 arms, and each one looks the same!

What are X-Rays?

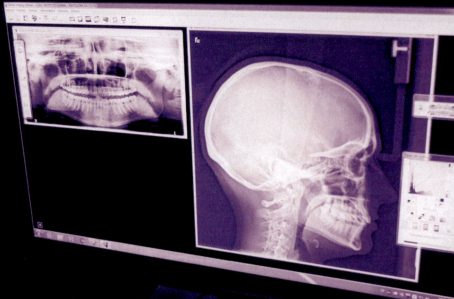

The full light spectrum is much larger than what our eyes can see. There are many kinds of light humans can't see at all. The light we can see is called **visible light**.

Light is a form of **electromagnetic radiation**, an energy that travels in the form of **electromagnetic waves**. On the radiation spectrum chart below, you see radio waves and microwaves, infrared light, ultraviolet light, X-rays, and Gamma rays. None of these rays are visible to us. See how narrow the visible light portion is?

The wavy line shows the wavelengths of different types of radiation. And you can also see that the hotter the object that radiates the light, the shorter the light wavelength. Radio waves are the coolest with the longest wavelength, while gamma rays are the hottest with the shortest wavelength.

visible light

| radio | microwave | infrared | visible | ultraviolet | X-ray | Gamma ray |

cooler → hotter

Rays of shorter wavelengths have higher-energy photons.
X-rays are some of the highest-energy rays. Sunlight, a 'visible light' on our chart, bounces off your skin because its energy is low.
But X-ray photons are so energetic, they go right through your skin,
and will only bounce off thicker portions of your body, such as your bones or teeth.

That's why when they make an X-ray picture of a person's body at the doctor's office, the picture shows the bones, but no muscles or skin. Very useful if someone has a broken arm or a problem with a tooth!

At the airport our suitcases are passed through X-ray machines. The machines show what's inside each suitcase. Security officers look at the X-ray machine screen to make sure nobody has a weapon or any other dangerous object in their bag.

What is a Laser?

Where are laser beams on the chart of light? Laser beams may be visible or invisible. They can be anywhere from infrared light to ultraviolet light. And, of course, many laser beams are visible light, because we can see them. . So what makes laser beams different from other light?

The word **laser** is made from the first letters of this long name:
Light Amplification by the Stimulated Emission of Radiation
The word *amplify* means to make something bigger and stronger. There is no laser light in nature. Lasers are man-made, or **artificial**. They are sharper and stronger than natural light.

Laser beams are used in light shows, in eye surgery, and in many devices and machines.

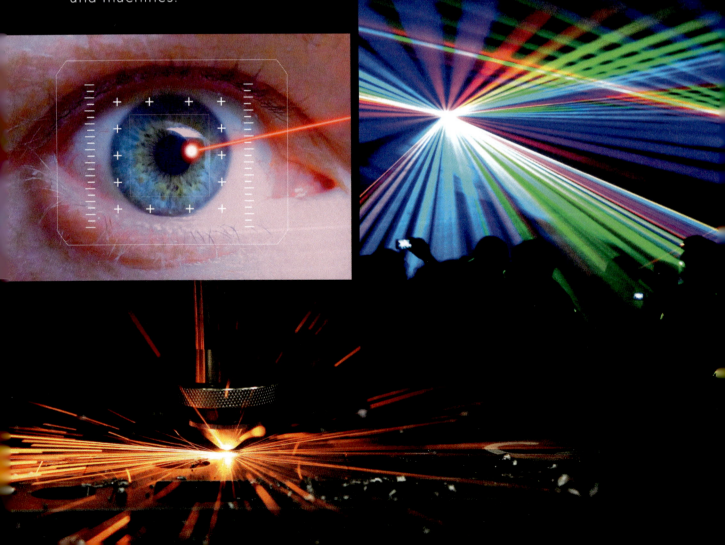

In natural light, such as sunlight, each photon has its own path and moves on its own. Its direction and wavelength can be slightly different from those of other photons around. But in a laser beam all photons have the same wavelength. They move 'in step,' in exactly the same direction.
That's what makes laser light so sharp, precise, and powerful.

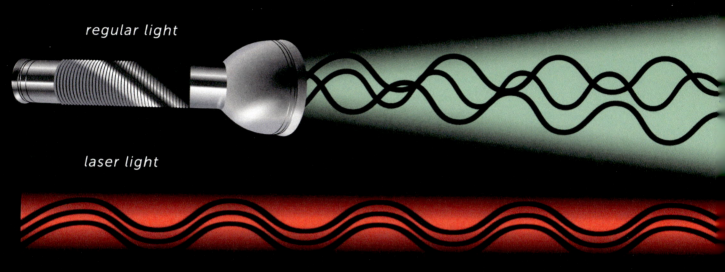

regular light

laser light

The simplest laser beam device can be a cylinder, filled with helium and neon gases. The cylinder has mirrors on its ends. One of the mirrors is partially transparent, and allows some photons to escape.

When light shines into the cylinder, it bounces back and forth between the mirrors. The atoms of helium and neon become excited and release more and more photons. The photons form a beam in which all photons have the same wavelength and move in step. The beam grows stronger and sharper, and escapes through the partially transparent mirror.

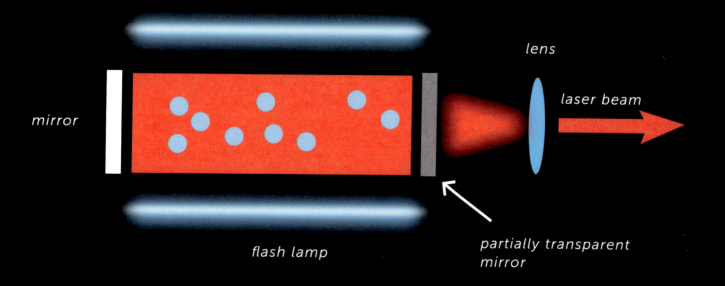

Why is Glass Transparent?

not transparent

Transparent means you can see through it.
Window glass is transparent.
How is window glass different from paper or wood which are not transparent?

Visible light can't go through things without getting either absorbed or reflected.

If the light is reflected by an object, we see that object colored with the color of the reflected light - not transparent.

If the light is absorbed by an object, we see it as black or dark - not transparent. When absorbed, or 'eaten up' by an object, light photons turn into heat.
That's why things warm up and even get hot if left in the sunlight.

So what makes things transparent?

not transparent

transparent

Here is how glass works.

Everything is made of molecules. **Molecules** are made of **atoms**, and inside an atom **electrons** revolve around the **nucleus**, or atom center, forming a cloud of energy.

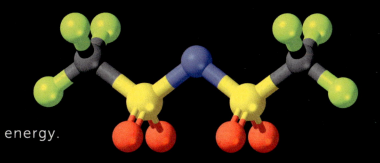

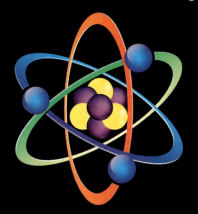

The electrons need energy to keep the atom together, but not too much energy, and not too little energy - just the right amount.

Electrons in the atoms that make glass are very energy-hungry, but they are picky eaters. They eat — absorb — light photons, but only the high-energy ones.

For example, ultraviolet, or UV, light photons are very high-energy, so glass absorbs them and stops UV light.

But the photons of visible light, such as sunlight, don't have enough energy, so the glass atoms are not interested in them. Glass atoms first absorb them, and then instantly spit them out, letting them continue on their path. That's how visible light goes through glass — and we see glass as transparent.

visible light

ultraviolet light

Why Do We Get a Suntan?

Why does our skin becomes darker when we spend time in the bright sun? A suntan is caused by ultraviolet (also called UV) rays of light.

There are 2 kinds of UV rays that reach our skin - UVA and UVB. UVB rays hit the top layer of our skin and cause sunburns.
But it's the UVA rays that make people tan. UVA rays get deeper into our skin. They can damage skin cells - the tiny building blocks of our skin. Skin cells defend themselves from UVA rays by producing melanin. Melanin is the brown 'dye' that makes us look tanned.

Darker-skinned people come from parts of the world the sun is high in the sky more of the year. They are darker because their skin produces more melanin. A suntan may be pretty, but spending a lot of time in the sun is not good for you. UVA rays can cause skin diseases, and they also make our skin look dry, tired, and wrinkly.

How Do Mirrors Work?

One of the laws of nature is **conservation of energy**:

Energy can't appear from nothing,
or disappear without a trace.

So when photons of light,
which are tiny bundles of energy, hit an object, where do they go?
They can • pass through an object,
  • sink into it and heat it up with their energy,
  • or bounce off.

A mirror has 3 layers: • transparent glass on top
  • shiny silvery material in the middle, like aluminum
  • and a protective layer of paint at the bottom.

Photons of light reach the silvery layer of the mirror and sink into the atoms of aluminum. Electrons in the atoms of aluminum are excited by the energy of the photons, become unstable, and spit the photons out.

The photons leave the mirror at the same angle,
but in a different direction, forming a V-shaped path,
just like a ball that hits the wall and bounces off.

photon

aluminum atom

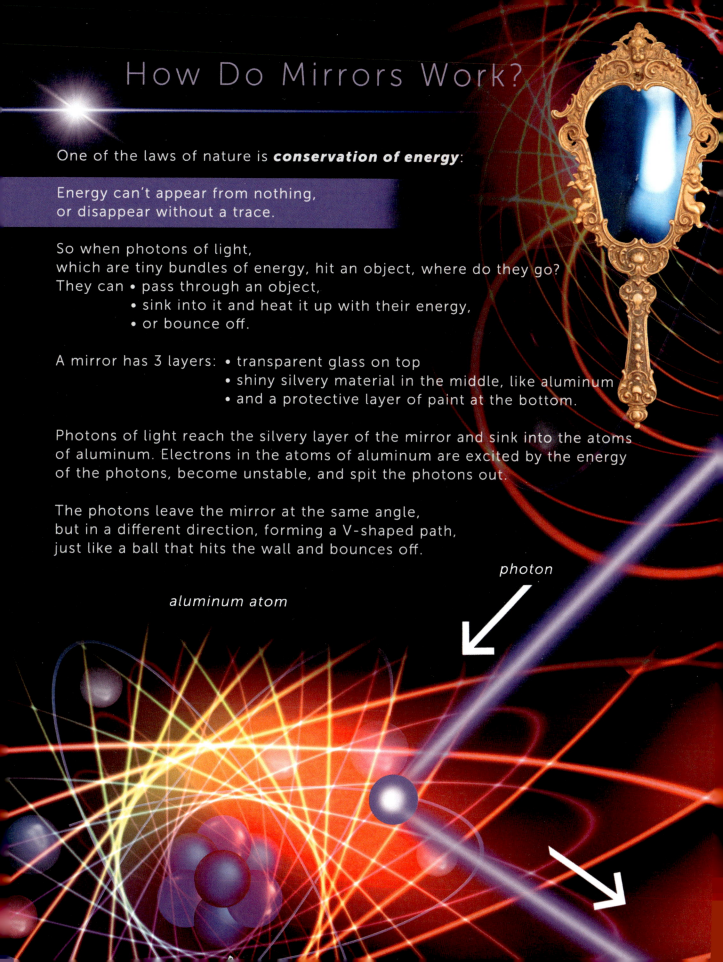

Why Don't Oil and Water Mix?

Molecules of different substances have different structures. Some molecules have opposite poles, like batteries, with opposite electrical charges - plus and minus. Such molecules are called **polar.**

Water molecules are polar. They have a **V** shape, with 2 hydrogen atoms at the ends, and 1 oxygen atom at the bottom of the V. The **chemical formula** of water is H_2O where H_2 = 2 hydrogen atoms and **O** = 1 oxygen atom. Chemical formulas like H_2O show which atoms make a molecule.

The bottom of the V has a negative charge, while the top ends of the V have a positive electrical charge.

Because they are polar, water molecules are attracted to one another. The ends of one V chase the tip of another V. They stack together and don't let in any non-polar molecules.

Oil molecules are non-polar. They don't have plus and minus electrical charges on opposite ends. And that's the reason they can't mix with water molecules.

How Does Soap Work?

So oil won't dissolve in water. If you pour oil into water, it will end up floating on top, unmixed with water. But soap clearly can do something to oil. That's why we use soap - somehow it breaks down oil. Soap helps us fight dirt, and clean food off of our dishes.
How does soap work?

While water molecules are polar and oil molecules are non-polar, soap molecules are polar on one end, and non-polar on the other end!

That's why they can make friends with both, oil and water! Their head dissolves in water and their tail dissolves in oil.

When you pour some dish soap on an oily dish, each soap molecule turns itself so that
its polar end is pointing at water molecules, and its non-polar end is pointing at oil molecules.

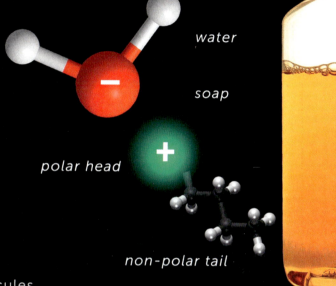

Soap molecules are chasing water molecules with their polar head, while reaching for oil molecules with their non-polar tail. This breaks oil into tiny drops, and each drop gets coated with soap molecules. Finally oil gets completely hidden inside these soap bubbles, and all you have to do is flush soap and oil with water, and your dish is clean!

oil surrounded with soap molecules

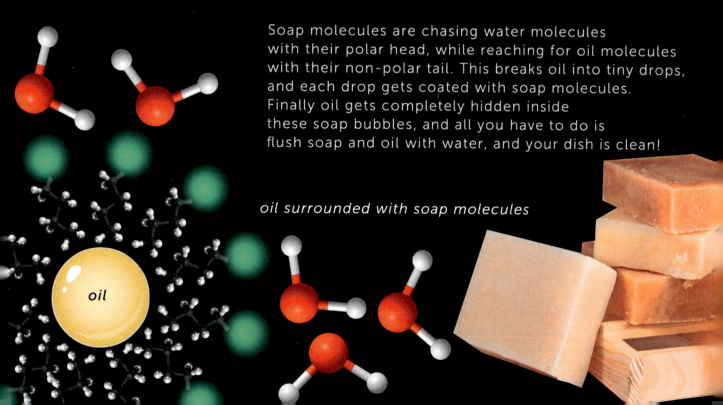

Why Does Ice Take More Space Than Water?

Fill an ice tray with water and put it in the freezer. If your tray is really full, when the water freezes you will see that the ice rises above the top of the tray. There is more of the ice than there was of the water. Why?

Again, the secret is the polar structure of water molecules. Because they have a plus and a minus electrical charge at opposite ends, water molecules are attracted to each other.
When water is liquid, the molecules are moving all the time. They bond, or stick together, then fall apart, then bond again. But when water freezes, its molecules stop moving and line up in a way that all the hydrogen atoms are as close to all the oxygen atoms as possible. To make this happen, they form a six-sided shape. And that leaves a lot of empty space in the middle!

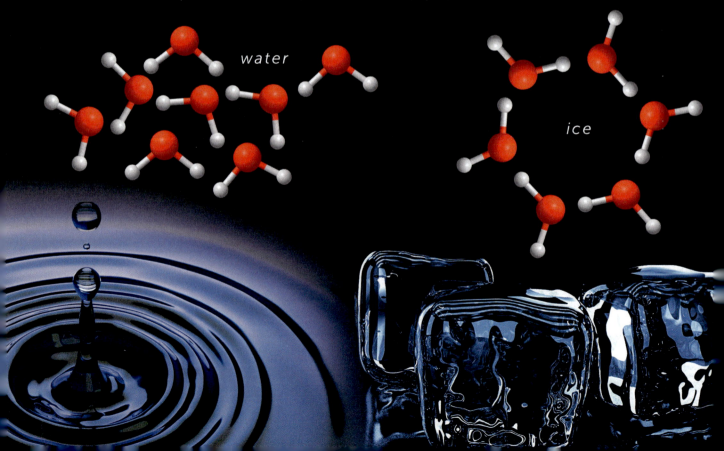

water

ice

That's why ice takes up more room than water.
And that's why snowflakes have 6 arms –
they grow from 6-sided shapes water molecules
form when water freezes.

In water, molecules are closer to each other.
In ice, they are farther apart. So water is more **dense** than ice.
Density is how much stuff you can put in a unit of space.
Because water is more dense, you can always fit
more water than ice into a cup.

That's also why ice floats on water! Look at this iceberg!
If an object is more dense than water, it will sink.
If an object is less dense than water,
it will float.

iceberg

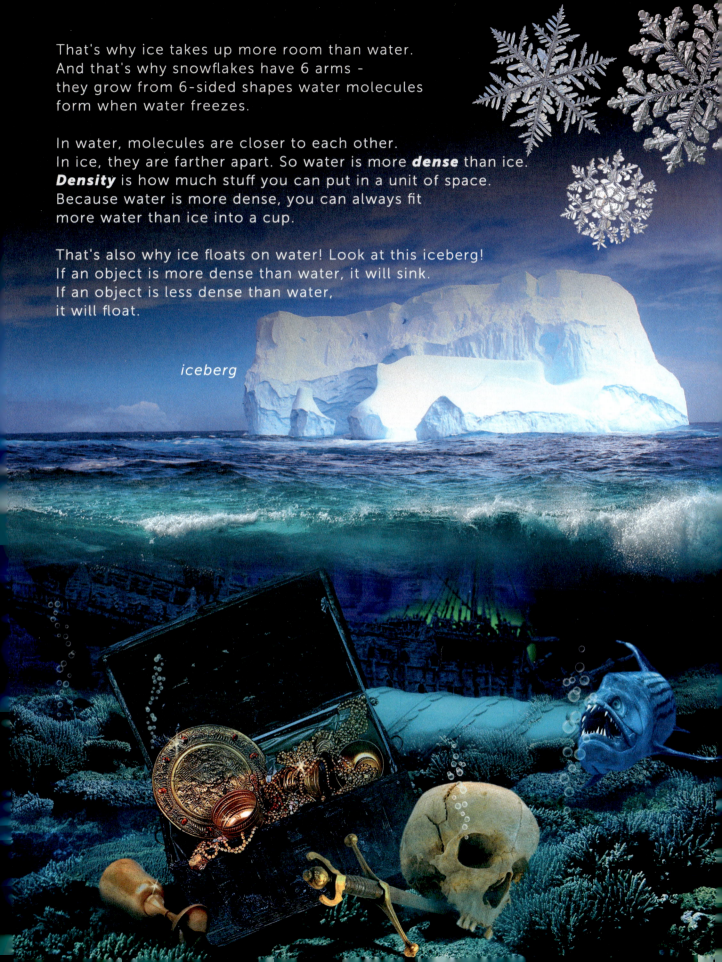

Why Do Hot Air Balloons Fly?

Any substance can exist in 3 different states:

If you heat up a solid substance, such as ice, its molecules will wiggle out of their fixed order. The ice will melt and turn into a liquid - water.

If you heat up that water, its molecules will start moving even faster, scatter around, and the water will turn into a gas – water vapor.

In water vapor molecules are farther apart than in water. It is less dense than air, and when the water is boiling, the vapor rises up.

A hot air balloon has a burner that heats up the air inside the balloon. Because it is less dense than the air outside the balloon, the hot air rises up and lifts the balloon into the sky.

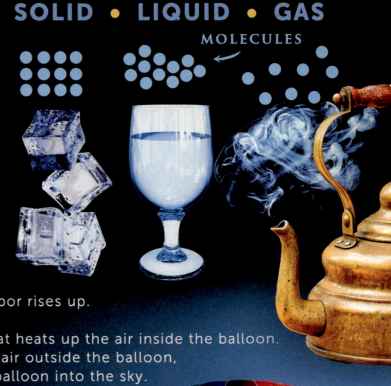

SOLID • LIQUID • GAS

MOLECULES

Why Don't Oceans Freeze in Winter?

Ponds, lakes, and rivers often freeze in winter, but oceans don't. Why?

One reason is that oceans are so huge and store so much heat, it would take them a really long time to cool to the point of freezing. Another reason is that there is too much movement in the oceans. There are all those waves, tides, and water currents rushing back and forth.

And there is one more reason. It's that oceans are salty, and salty water freezes at a lower temperature than regular fresh water.

The temperature of freezing is called the **freezing point**. The freezing point of fresh water is 0° Celsius or 32° Fahrenheit. But the freezing point of salty ocean water is -1.8° C or 28.8° F. Why?

A molecule of salt is made of
1 atom of **sodium** and 1 atom of **chlorine**.
Its chemical formula is **NaCl**.
When salt is dissolved in water,
its molecules separate into an atom
of sodium that has a positive electrical charge, and an atom
of chlorine that has a negative electrical charge.
These atoms chase water molecules,
which have both positive and negative
electrical charges, and don't let them
line up into those 6-sided shapes
that make ice. This slows down
the freezing of salt water,
lowering its freezing point.

What about icebergs? They are pieces of glaciers which are made of rainwater. What about Arctic ice? Fresh rainwater!

Why Are Bubbles Round?

Bubbles are round, and so are drops of water. Why? Is there an invisible balloon skin around bubbles and drops of water that somehow holds them together?

When you make a soap bubble, air is trapped inside the bubble 'skin.' Air molecules are moving inside the bubble and pushing on this soap 'skin.' This pushing, or pressure, is the same in all directions. This helps the bubble to stay round.

Another reason bubbles are round is **surface tension**. What is surface tension?

Molecules are held together by a bond, a special force that makes them stick to one another like magnets. Because of this force, the soap molecules all around the bubble are trying to stay as close together as possible. Round, the shape of a ball, is the most compact shape in nature. **Compact** means packing more stuff into less space. The roundness of a bubble allows the soap molecules to stay as close together as possible. That's why soap bubbles are round!

Surface tension is what makes drops of water round too. Inside a drop, water molecules are surrounded by other water molecules and they all try to stay as close together as they can. But on the surface of a drop, water molecules have air on one side, and water on the other side. So they try to move toward the center of the drop, running away from the air molecules. And that's what holds a drop of water together and makes it round.

And why are bubbles rainbow-colored? That is because light waves reflected from the opposite walls of the bubble run into each other. Some light waves cancel each other, and others grow, and the light stops being white - we start seeing beautiful colors.

Why Do Fizzy Drinks Fizz?

Fizzy drinks are also called **carbonated** drinks. 'Carbonated' means they have **carbon dioxide** in them.

Carbon dioxide is a gas found in the Earth's atmosphere. When we breathe, we inhale oxygen from the air and exhale carbon dioxide. Plants absorb carbon dioxide from the air and use it for growth.

carbon dioxide molecule

OXYGEN CYCLE

PLANTS ABSORB ENERGY FROM LIGHT

PLANTS RELEASE OXYGEN

PEOPLE AND ANIMALS BREATHE IN OXYGEN

PEOPLE AND ANIMALS BREATHE OUT CARBON DIOXIDE

PLANTS ABSORB CARBON DIOXIDE

Solid carbon dioxide is known as **dry ice**. It's used to keep food cold and scare you on Halloween. At room temperature dry ice turns into a liquid and then into a gas. It cools the air around it and causes water vapor in the air to condense into a thick fog.

To make a drink fizzy, molecules of carbon dioxide are forced into the drink and sealed up tight in a bottle or can. The molecules of carbon dioxide are squished together and push hard on the walls of the bottle trying to set themselves free. This creates pressure inside the bottle and does not allow carbon dioxide to form bubbles.
That's why there are no bubbles in a carbonated drink until you open the bottle. Once you open it, the pressure is gone, and the carbon dioxide rushes to the surface of your drink in tiny bubbles that escape into the atmosphere.

If you shake a sealed fizzy drink, carbon dioxide trapped between the drink and the top of the can is pushed into the drink. When you open the can, the drink fizzes and foams and often spills out! That happens because the drink gets so filled with carbon dioxide that its bubbles force the drink right out of the can!

Why Does Metal Feel Colder than Plastic?

Different materials differ in their ability to conduct, or guide the flow of heat. If an object can heat up and cool off real fast, it is good at **conducting heat**. It has good **thermal conductivity**.

Metals are excellent heat conductors, that's why metal objects often feel cold to the touch. Since room temperature is lower than your body temperature, metal quickly absorbs the heat from your hand, making it feel cold. This is also why hot metal can burn you so easily. It transfers its heat into your skin very fast.

Plastic is not good at conducting heat. So things made of plastic don't take away the heat of your hand. That's why plastic feels warmer to the touch.

Many metal pots and pans have plastic handles to protect your hands from getting burned.

The best heat conductors at room temperature are diamonds, silver, gold, and copper.

copper electric wire

How do clothes keep you warm? What warms you is the air between your clothes and your skin. Air is bad at conducting heat. So the layer of air between your shirt and your body seals the heat of your body and doesn't allow it to escape outside your shirt. Think of it as a shirt made of air under your regular shirt!

So what is warmer: 3 light shirts or 1 thick shirt? 3 light shirts, because there are 3 layers of air - or 3 air shirts! - between the 3 light shirts, but only 1 layer of air under 1 thick shirt.

Does Air Have Weight?

heavy

Some things are heavy and some things are light. Why?

The Earth is like a huge magnet. It pulls everything on and around it downward toward its center. This pulling force is called **gravity**. Gravity gives weight to things.

light

OK, so does air have weight?
Sure. The force of gravity pulls the molecules of air down, just as it pulls down everything else.
The air that fits in a jar or a bottle doesn't weigh much. But think of all the air above your head – from the top of your head to the top of the Earth's atmosphere.

heavy? light?

Does air press down on you with its weight?
Yes! Air puts a pressure of 14.7 pounds on every square inch of your body!
A square inch is a square with 1-inch sides like this:

1 inch

1 inch   1 inch

1 inch

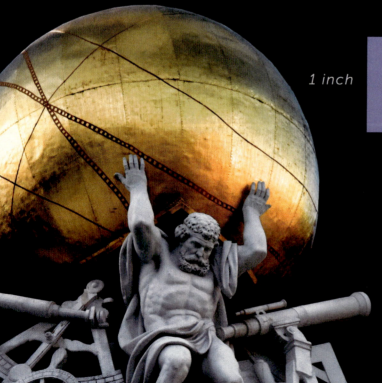

In ancient Greece they believed that the sky was solid and that it was held up by Atlas, one of the giant Titans.

Now we know that the sky is the atmosphere of the Earth. But the myth about Atlas is right in one way: The sky, or the air above us, is heavy!

100 meters above sea level →

sea level →

What if you climb
a high mountain?
The weight of the air
over you will be less.
There are two reasons for this.
1. High on the mountain there will be less air between the top of your head and the top of the Earth's atmosphere.
2. The higher you go, the less dense the air becomes. It's lighter because its molecules are farther apart.

Scientists use the words **sea level** to describe places that are low.
So at sea level, the pressure of air on a square inch of your body is 14.7 pounds.
But in the mountains it can be as little as half of that - 7.4 pounds!

When you are in the mountains, you may feel differently.
The air pressure is less, so maybe you feel lighter.
But because the air is less thick, you also breathe in less oxygen.
That's why in the mountains you can feel dizzy or get tired real fast.

Why Do Helium Balloons Float in the Air?

All things around us are made of molecules, and molecules are made of atoms. Let's remember what goes on inside an atom.

At the center of an atom is the **nucleus**, the core of the atom, made of **protons** and **neutrons**.
Protons are tiny particles that carry a positive (+) electrical charge.
Neutrons have no electrical charge, they are neutral.
The nucleus is surrounded by a cloud of moving **electrons**.
Electrons are particles that carry negative (-) electrical charge.
They move around the nucleus in **shells**, or orbits.

Each atom has an equal number of protons and electrons, but that number is different for different substances, or **chemical elements.**
That number is called the **Atomic Number**.

All chemical elements can be arranged in a table, called the **Periodic Table.**

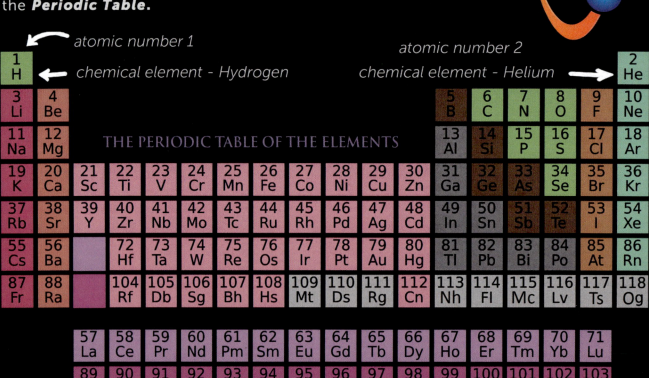

atomic number 1 ← chemical element - Hydrogen

atomic number 2 — chemical element - Helium →

THE PERIODIC TABLE OF THE ELEMENTS

The first element in the table
has the smallest atomic number, 1.
This element is **Hydrogen**.
Hydrogen has 1 proton and 1 electron.
There is a lot of hydrogen in the air,
and also water is made partially from hydrogen.
Remember, the chemical formula of water is H_2O,
which means a molecule of water has 2 atoms of hydrogen
and 1 atom of oxygen.

Because of its tiny atomic number, hydrogen is the lightest element.
If you fill a balloon with hydrogen, it will rise up into the air,
because pure hydrogen is lighter than air.

The second lightest chemical element is Helium.
Its atomic number is 2. It has 2 protons and 2 electrons.
Helium balloons float, because pure helium is also lighter than air!

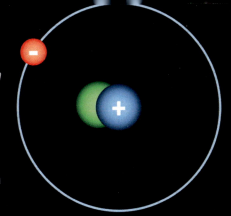
hydrogen atom

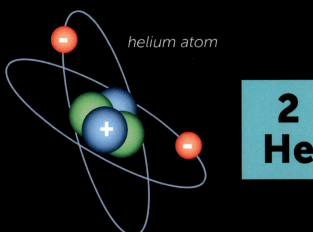
helium atom

*A blimp, or dirigible, is a helium-filled balloon with tail fins and an engine.
Blimps are used to display advertising messages.*

What is Fire?

Fire, or burning, is a chemical reaction in which fuel reacts with oxygen making heat and light.

The scientific name for this reaction is **combustion.**

An oxygen atom has 8 electrons. Its atomic number is 8. It also has two extra spaces for two more electrons. It doesn't like having these empty spaces, and always tries to bond with other chemical elements to borrow some electrons from them.

Oxygen can bond with almost any chemical element. Scientists call it a **reactive** element, because it is always looking for a chemical reaction that will give it some extra electrons.

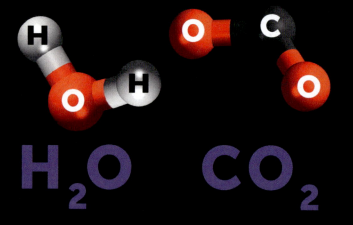

H_2O CO_2

Chemical reactions create new substances.
So when a piece of paper is burning, oxygen is reacting with carbon in the paper and hydrogen in the air. Oxygen bonds with the molecules of carbon and hydrogen, and creates water H_2O, and carbon dioxide, CO_2.

CO_2 is the chemical formula of carbon dioxide. It shows that a carbon dioxide molecule has one atom of carbon and 2 atoms of oxygen.

As burning happens, the energy of oxygen, hydrogen, and carbon is released in the form of heat and light photons.

Why Won't Water Burn?

Water is what you get when you burn hydrogen.

The water molecule **H₂O** is made of 2 atoms of hydrogen and one atom of oxygen. Both hydrogen and oxygen are real champions when it comes to burning! They are constantly looking for trouble and burn very easily. If you combine hydrogen and oxygen and add some heat to start burning, you'll get fire and water.

Fire is energy escaping in the form of heat and light. Once the energy is gone, oxygen and hydrogen are tied up into molecules of water, and water doesn't have any energy left to burn.

What makes hydrogen such a troublemaker?
Each hydrogen molecule is made of 2 atoms of hydrogen. But each atom has only 1 electron, so the hydrogen molecule can easily fall apart. Hydrogen atoms are always looking for a new molecule to join, and because of that, hydrogen easily combines with other elements to form new substances.

Here is how you can write down the chemical reaction of hydrogen burning:

$$2H_2 + O_2 \rightarrow 2H_2O$$

2H₂ is 2 molecules of hydrogen, each made of 2 hydrogen atoms. These hydrogen molecules join **O₂**
O₂ is a molecule of oxygen made of 2 oxygen atoms.
As a result you get **2H₂O** – 2 molecules of water.

What is Electricity?

Electricity is a movement of electrons from atom to atom.
An atom can lose one or more of its electrons.
When an atom loses an electron, that electron is free
and it starts looking for a new atom to join.
It finds a new atom and bumps an electron from it
to make space for itself. The electron that was kicked out
of its atom starts looking for a new atom too!
That's how electrons travel along an electric wire.

Some materials lose electrons easily, and make great electrical conductors.
A **conductor** is a material that guides - conducts - a flow of electric current.

The best conductors are copper, silver, and gold.

Materials whose atoms will not easily let go of their electrons
are called **insulators**. They stop the flow of electrons.

Glass, rubber, plastic, and air are all great insulators.

An electric battery has two ends, or poles –
a plus or **positive** pole and
a minus or **negative** pole.
Chemical reactions inside the battery make atoms lose electrons.
So if you connect the two poles of the battery with an electric wire,

How Does Lightning Happen?

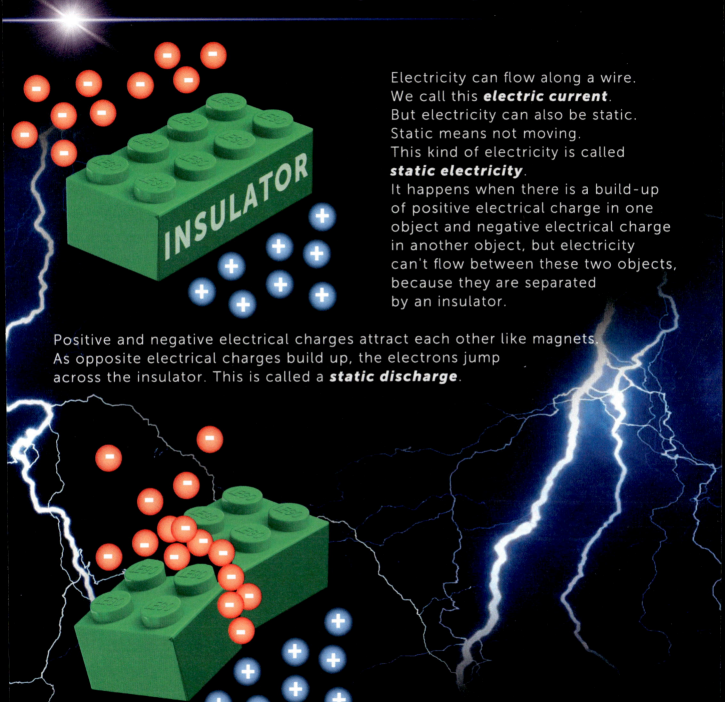

Electricity can flow along a wire. We call this **electric current**. But electricity can also be static. Static means not moving. This kind of electricity is called **static electricity**. It happens when there is a build-up of positive electrical charge in one object and negative electrical charge in another object, but electricity can't flow between these two objects, because they are separated by an insulator.

Positive and negative electrical charges attract each other like magnets. As opposite electrical charges build up, the electrons jump across the insulator. This is called a **static discharge**.

Lightning is a static discharge. Groups of clouds build up opposite electrical charges. Or opposite charges build up in the clouds and on the ground below. Finally the static discharge happens. A stream of free electrons rushes through the air, bumping into the atoms of the air, and giving up energy as flashes of light — lightning!

Why Does Iron Rust?

What causes iron to rust?
It's that troublemaker oxygen again!
All you need to make iron rust
is iron and water, and you'll get brown soft stuff we call 'rust'.
Its scientific name is **iron oxide**, which means iron combined with oxygen.

When water hits iron,
some water molecules separate
into oxygen and hydrogen.
Free oxygen atoms start
chasing the atoms of iron.
Atoms of iron give some electrons
to the atoms of oxygen,
and they join together into molecules of iron oxide.

The chemical symbol of iron is **Fe**.
The Latin word **ferrum** means iron.
The formula of iron oxide is **Fe_2O_3** –
2 atoms of iron and 3 atoms of oxygen.

Not all metals rust. Iron rusts. Steel rusts, because it has iron in it. But aluminum doesn't rust. Some other metals that don't rust are gold, platinum, and stainless steel.

Some metals, such as copper or brass, react with oxygen in the air and form a layer of blue-green oxide on top. We call that layer **tarnish**.

iron oxide molecule

a brass door knocker

a brass button

Soft drink cans are made of aluminum. They don't rust.

The Statue of Liberty is made of copper. Its copper layer is as thick as two pennies put together.

Plants create energy for their growth through a process called photosynthesis.
Photosynthesis is a chemical reaction.
It turns light energy into chemical energy.

How do plants make photosynthesis happen?

They
- absorb water H_2O from the soil
- capture the energy of sunlight using **chlorophyll**, the green pigment in their leaves
- absorb carbon dioxide, CO_2 from the air.

During photosynthesis plants use the energy of sunlight to split molecules of water H_2O into hydrogen and oxygen.
They also use carbon dioxide CO_2 to make carbohydrates.

Carbohydrates are sugar molecules in which plants store energy. In summer carbohydrates are stored in leaves. In the fall plants move their carbohydrates into their branches and roots.

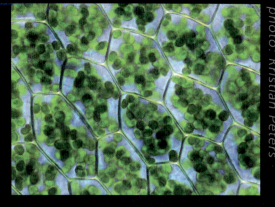

chlorophyll under the microscope

photo: Kristian Peters

Why is a Candle Flame Yellow?

What is a flame? The flame is a visible portion of fire.

A candle is made of wax with a wick in the middle. The wick is a piece of string. As it burns, the flame melts the wax. The wax burns too. The wax and the wick are fuel that candles burn.

Candle flame is blue near the wick, darker orange in the middle, and bright yellow on the outside and on the top. Why?

As the wick and wax burn, tiny burning bits of carbon fly up like sparks, glowing orange and yellow. That's what gives candle flame its yellow color.

To burn, fire needs oxygen. It gets oxygen from the air. If you put a jar over a burning candle, the fire will die once it burns all the oxygen in the jar. The flame sucks in oxygen from the air. The outside of the flame gets more oxygen, and the middle of the flame gets less oxygen. That's why candle flame is brighter on the outside, and darker in the middle.

invisible zone 1400°C

carbon sparks

luminous zone 1200°C

blue zone 800°C

dark zone 1000°C

Today most candles are made from paraffin wax, but in ancient times all candles were made from real beeswax like this.

Why is the flame blue nearest to the wick? Because that's where the burning is happening. The energy is the highest there.

Match flame looks very much like candle flame. Carbon sparks from burning wood color it orange and yellow.
But what about gas stove burners? Their flame is blue!

A gas stove burner burns natural gas. There are no carbon sparks from wick or wood flying into the flame, and nothing to glow orange or yellow. That's why the gas flame is pure blue.

Only when a piece of food you are cooking falls into the flame, do we see a flash of yellow-orange light.

And why does a flame always point up?
That's because it heats up the air around it. Hot air rises up, because it is less dense than cold air. The stream of rising hot air keeps the flame pointing up.

Diamonds and Graphite

The inside portion of a pencil is called a lead (sounds like 'led'). The lead is what puts marks on paper, and it's made from graphite.

Graphite is made of carbon.

But diamonds are also made of carbon! How can the soft tip of your pencil, and a diamond, which is one of the hardest substances on Earth, be made of the same stuff? Yet, it's true. Diamond and graphite are both made entirely of carbon atoms. What makes them different is how carbon atoms are arranged inside diamond and graphite.

In diamonds each carbon atom is connected to 4 other atoms. They form a strong 3-dimensional structure. But in graphite each carbon atom is bonded to only 3 other atoms, and they form layers with a lot of space between them. That's why diamond is hard and graphite is soft.

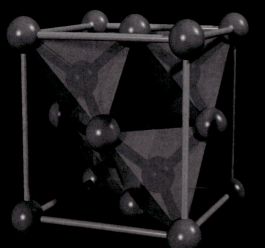

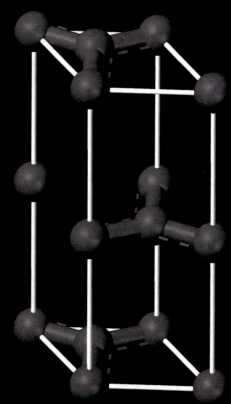

Made in the USA
San Bernardino, CA
28 January 2020